THE COMPLETE PLANT-BASED COOKBOOK

Table of Contents

Introduction

Congratulations on purchasing your copy of *The Complete Plant-Based Cookbook*. I am delighted that you have chosen to take the path of bettering your health through plant-based cooking. Plant-based cooking is a nutritional avenue that allows you to appreciate food in its uncultivated, raw form. The goal of this cookbook is to introduce you to delicious plant-based recipes that are as satisfying as the not-so-healthy comfort foods we have all become so easily addicted to. As daunting as this new cooking lifestyle may be, you will find that these mouth-watering recipes will soon become the new favorite staples in your household.

In Chapter 1, you will notice that the main dishes will require a few more steps to prepare. However, each recipe will provide you with an estimated preparation and cooking time. You will also see the number of servings each recipe can yield, along with its nutritional values, which include the net carbohydrates, protein, fats, and calories. The guesswork has been eliminated for your convenience—unless you want to get creative and add some extra ingredients of your own! The remainder of the book is chock-full of easy-to-follow recipes that will require very little work for highly delicious outcomes.

There are plenty of books on plant-based cooking out there, so thanks again for choosing this one! Every effort was made to ensure that it is full of as much useful information as possible. As always, before implementing any major diet change such as this one, please consult a physician and ensure any questions concerning your nutritional health are answered.

BONUS:

As a way of saying thank you for purchasing my book, please use your link below to claim your 3 FREE Cookbooks on Health, Fitness & Dieting Instantly

https://bit.ly/2MkqTit

You can also share your link with your friends and families whom you think that can benefit from the cookbooks or you can forward them the link as a gift!

Chapter 1: Main Dishes

Portobello Bruschetta

10 Min. to Get Ready | 5 Min. to Cook
Produces: 4 Servings
Nutritional Score: Calories: 284 | Net Carbs: 13.3 g | Fat: 25.7 g | Protein: 5.4 g

Ingredients:

- ½ C. olive oil
- 6 chopped tomatoes
- 1 C. chopped basil
- 12 cloves minced garlic
- 4 portobello mushrooms
- Salt and pepper

Technique:

1. Take 2 T. of oil and 4 cloves of minced garlic to coat each mushroom. Cook in a grilling pan for 5 minutes on each side.
2. Mix up tomatoes, basil, remaining garlic, and oil. Fill each mushroom. Top with salt and pepper.

Baked Vegetable Foil Packs

20 Min. to Get Ready | 20 Min. to Cook
Produces: 4 Servings
Nutritional Score: Calories: 97 | Net Carbs: 8 g | Fat: 7.3 g | Protein: 2.3 g

Ingredients:

- 1 peeled and chopped onion
- 1 cut-up yellow squash
- 1 sliced zucchini
- 2 T. olive oil
- Spices of choice

Technique:

1. In a bowl, mix all ingredients with olive oil; add spices of choice and toss together.
2. Wrap ingredients in foil; make 4 individual packets.
3. Cook at 350°F for 20 minutes.

Sweet Potato and Black Bean Tacos

15 Min. to Get Ready | 20 Min. to Cook
Produces: 4 Servings
Nutritional Score: Calories: 430 | Net Carbs: 60 g | Fat: 16 g |
Protein: 12 g

Ingredients:

- 4 C. sweet potatoes – no skin, cut in 1" squares
- 1 C. black beans – canned or cooked
- 1 chopped onion
- 2 T. olive oil
- 8 corn tortillas
- 3 minced garlic cloves
- Cilantro

Technique:

1. Heat olive oil and add in sweet potatoes. Cook for about 5-6 minutes. Periodically stir.
2. Add in onion, garlic, and black beans, cover and let cook for another 10-15 minutes, or until sweet potatoes are at desired readiness.
3. Serve in warmed corn tortillas; top with cilantro.

Avocado and White Bean Sandwich

5 Min. to Get Ready | 5 Min. to Cook
Produces: 3 Servings
Nutritional Score: Calories: 325 | Net Carbs: 44.5 g | Fat: 13.1 g |
Protein: 9.8 g

Ingredients:

- 1 avocado
- 1 15-oz. can clean white beans
- Juice from 1 lemon
- 1 T. Dijon mustard
- Optional: greens and cherry tomatoes
- Salt and pepper

Technique:

1. Drain and clean beans.
2. Mash avocado and beans together; add in the rest of the ingredients.
3. Spoon onto romaine leaves or gluten-free whole wheat bread.

Veggie-Loaded Rice Bowls

20 Min. to Get Ready | 30 Min. to Cook
Produces: 4 Servings
Nutritional Score: Calories: 547 | Net Carbs: 106.4 g | Fat: 2.1 g |
Protein: 26.6 g

Ingredients:

- ½ C. chopped cilantro
- 1 C. pinto beans
- 1 C. black beans
- 1 C. cooked brown rice
- 3 C. spinach
- 1 cut-up zucchini
- 1 chopped bell pepper
- 1 chopped onion
- 1 lime
- 1 t. cumin
- 1 t. turmeric

Technique:

1. Sauté onion and bell pepper for 5 minutes. Add beans and zucchini; cook until warm. Put in your spinach and heat until wilted.
2. Add in cooked rice and spices; stir to combine.
3. Add some juice from a squeezed lime once finished.

Hummus Vegetable Wrap

10 Min. to Get Ready | 25 Min. to Cook
Produces: 4 Servings
Nutritional Score: Calories: 441 | Net Carbs: 68.1 g | Fat: 15.2 g |
Protein: 11.7 g

Ingredients:

- 4 whole wheat tortillas
- 1/2 C. hummus
- 4 C. spinach
- 1 cut-up avocado
- ½ thinly sliced cucumber
- 1 thinly sliced bell pepper
- 2-3 shredded carrots
- 1 can cleaned black beans
- 1 C. cooked brown rice

Technique:

1. Warm up your tortillas.
2. On each tortilla, spread a couple of tablespoons of hummus.
3. Top with your cooked rice and the remaining vegetables.

Zucchini Noodle Pasta with Avocado Pesto

15 Min. to Get Ready | 15 Min. to Cook
Produces: 8 Servings
Nutritional Score: Calories: 214 | Net Carbs: 13.2 g | Fat: 17.1 g | Protein: 4.8 g

Ingredients:

- 6 spiralized zucchinis
- 1 T. cold-pressed oil of choice

Avocado Pesto:

- 3 garlic cloves
- 2 cubed avocados
- 1 C. fresh basil leaves
- ¼ C. fresh parsley leaves
- ¼ C. pine nuts
- 3 T. cold-pressed oil of choice
- Juice from 1 lemon
- Salt and pepper

Technique:

1. Spiralize your zucchini and set aside on paper towels.
2. In a food processor, add in all the ingredients for the avocado pesto except the oil. Pulse on low until desired consistency is reached.
3. Slowly add in oil until it's creamy and emulsified.
4. Heat 1 T. of oil and allow your zucchini noodles to cook for 4 minutes.
5. Take your zucchini noodles and coat them with avocado pesto.

Turmeric Roasted Potatoes and Asparagus

10 Min. to Get Ready | 40 Min. to Cook
Produces: 4 Servings
Nutritional Score: Calories: 210 | Net Carbs: 26.4 g | Fat: 11.1 g |
Protein: 4.3 g

Ingredients:

- 11 chopped onion
- 1 lb. small red potatoes
- 1 bunch quartered asparagus
- 4 minced garlic cloves
- 2 T. turmeric
- Salt and pepper
- Cold-pressed oil

Technique:

1. Set your oven's temperature to 375°F to preheat.
2. In a dish that's oven-safe, toss the cut-up potatoes with 1 T. of oil and roast for 20 minutes.
3. In another bowl, add asparagus, onions, garlic cloves, turmeric, salt, and pepper. Toss with 1 T. of oil. Add to roasting dish with potatoes.
4. Until potatoes are tender, allow it to cook; it should take around 20 minutes.

Vegan Zucchini Boats

15 Min. to Get Ready | 40 Min. to Cook
Produces: 4 Servings
Nutritional Score: Calories: 228 | Net Carbs: 35.2 g | Fat: 7.4 g |
Protein: 8.5 g

Ingredients:

- 2 zucchinis
- 1 C. (2 med. ears) fresh corn kernels
- 1 chopped onion
- 1 can cleaned black beans
- 1 diced bell pepper
- 2 minced cloves of garlic
- 1 diced tomato
- 1 small batch chopped fresh cilantro
- ½ C. quinoa
- 1 ¼ C. vegetable stock
- 2 t.:
  - Ground cumin
  - Chili powder
  - Dried oregano
- 2 T. cold-pressed olive oil

Technique:

1. Set your oven's temperature to 425°F to preheat.
2. Slice both zucchinis lengthwise down the center and carve out the inside to form the "boats." Save the insides for later. Drizzle the zucchinis with olive oil until they're lightly coated; add a sprinkle of salt and pepper. Position the zucchinis facing down over the prepared baking sheet; place in the oven and cook for around 10-15 minutes.
3. Cook the quinoa in the vegetable stock.
4. In a skillet, stir-fry the onion with 1 T. of olive oil.
5. Add in the remaining vegetables and spices.
6. Add the quinoa to the vegetable mixture; remove from heat.

7. "Stuff" each zucchini boat and place in the oven until tops are browned, which will take about 5-10 minutes.

Tomato Basil Soup

15 Min. to Get Ready | 15 Min. to Cook
Produces: 4 Servings
Nutritional Score: Calories: 53 | Net Carbs: 11.6 g | Fat: 0.5 g |
Protein: 2.3 g

Ingredients:

- 1 handful fresh basil leaves
- 3 minced garlic cloves
- 2 15-oz. cans tomatoes – no skin and seeded
- 1 chopped onion
- Salt and pepper

Technique:

1. Sauté garlic and onions for 5 minutes; add in tomatoes.
2. Heat everything thoroughly; remove from heat once you see steam.
3. Add basil, salt, and pepper; transfer to a blender and blend until a soup-like consistency has been achieved.

Thai Peanut Tofu with Sautéed Vegetables

15 Min. to Get Ready | 40 Min. to Cook
Produces: 2 Servings
Nutritional Score: Calories: 834 | Net Carbs: 95.7 g | Fat: 42.3 g |
Protein: 24.8 g

Ingredients:

- 1 package pressed and rinsed extra firm tofu
- 1 sliced red onion
- 1 C. packed spinach
- 1 C. shredded carrots
- 1 chopped bell pepper
- 1-inch minced ginger
- 1 small head broccoli – chopped into florets
- 2 minced garlic cloves
- 1 C. quinoa
- 1 can coconut milk
- 2 T. soy sauce
- 1 T. red curry paste
- 1 T. rice vinegar
- 1 T. peanut butter
- 1 t. agave

Technique:

1. Preheat your oven to 400°F.
2. Bake tofu for 20 minutes.
3. Cook quinoa.
4. Sauté garlic, onions, carrots, broccoli, and red pepper for about 5 minutes.
5. Mix in the coconut milk, ginger, soy sauce, curry paste, peanut butter, agave, and rice vinegar. Cook for 5 more minutes.
6. Add the spinach and baked tofu and cook uncovered for 10 minutes.
7. Serve on a bed of quinoa.

Stuffed Peppers

10 Min. to Get Ready | 30 Min. to Cook
Produces: 4 Servings
Nutritional Score: Calories: 668 | Net Carbs: 123.1 g | Fat: 6.1 g |
Protein: 34.4 g

Ingredients:

- 1½ C. cooked quinoa
- 1 C. cooked corn
- 4 bell peppers
- 1 15-oz. can black beans

Technique:

1. Preheat oven to 350°F.
2. Combine quinoa, black beans, and corn.
3. Cut off the top and deseed each pepper, then "stuff" and place in a baking dish to cook for 30 minutes.

Chapter 2: Desserts

Dark Chocolate Covered Bananas

10 Min. to Get Ready | 35 Min. to Cook
Produces: 14 Servings
Nutritional Score: Calories: 176 | Net Carbs: 26.6 g | Fat: 8.8 g |
Protein: 2.5 g

Ingredients:

- 2 C. dark chocolate chips
- 7 bananas – ripe, cut in half
- ¼ C. almond butter
- 2 T. coconut oil
- 14 popsicle sticks
- Toppings of choice

Technique:

1. Insert a popsicle stick in each banana half, about midway through. Line a cooking sheet with parchment paper for the bananas.
2. Melt the coconut oil in a pan; add in the dark chocolate chips, stir until completely melted.
3. Dip each banana in chocolate, making sure to cover it in chocolate entirely. Place bananas on parchment paper.
4. Drizzle the bananas with almond butter, sprinkle with coconut, cashews, pistachios, or dried cherries.
5. Freeze for 35 minutes.

No-Bake Peanut Butter Cookies Drizzled with Dark Chocolate

15 Min. to Get Ready | 20 Min. to Cook
Produces: 4 Servings (12 cookies)
Nutritional Score: Calories: 235 | Net Carbs: 22 g | Fat: 16.3 g | Protein: 6 g

Ingredients:

- ½ C. dark chocolate chips
- ½ C. peanut butter
- 1 t. pure vanilla extract
- 2 t. coconut oil
- 1 C. dates
- 1 C. almond meal

Technique:

1. In a blender or food processor, add in peanut butter, almond meal, dates, and vanilla extract. Pulse until a smooth consistency is reached.
2. Form dough into 1-inch sized balls and place on a parchment paper-lined cooking sheet.
3. With a fork, press down and make a crisscross pattern.
4. Melt together coconut oil and the dark chocolate chips. Drizzle each cookie with chocolate.
5. Place in the fridge until firm.

Vegan Pineapple Ice Cream

10 Min. to Get Ready | 3 Hr. Freeze Time
Produces: 4 Servings
Nutritional Score: Calories: 460 | Net Carbs: 56.9 g | Fat: 8.2 g |
Protein: 41.1 g

Ingredients:

- 1 C. Greek yogurt
- 3 C. frozen pineapple chunks

Technique:

1. Add Greek yogurt and pineapple chunks to a blender and run until smooth.
2. In a freezer-safe container, store until it's frozen.

Matcha & Coconut Power Bars

20 Min. to Get Ready | 45 Min. Freeze Time
Produces: 8 Bars
Nutritional Score: Calories: 430 | Net Carbs: 57.3 g | Fat: 20.9 g |
Protein: 11 g

Ingredients:

- 1 T. matcha powder + more for sprinkling
- 2 T. cacao nibs – unsweetened
- ½ C. raw almonds
- ½ C. pecans
- ¼ C. coconut flakes – unsweetened
- 1 ¼ C. pitted and roughly chopped dates
- 1/3 C. hemp seeds
- 1 t. agave

Technique:

1. In a food processor, combine 2 t. of matcha powder, agave, hemp seeds, pecans, almonds, and dates. Pulse until well-combined. The mixture should stick together like dough. If not, add more dates until it does.
2. Add cacao nibs until dispersed.
3. Line a baking sheet with parchment paper. Use hands to press mixture down until smooth.
4. Sprinkle with coconut flakes and extra matcha powder.
5. Freeze for 45 minutes.

Cashew Whipped Cream with Berries

15 Min. to Get Ready | 1 Hr. Cook Time
Produces: 4 Servings
Nutritional Score: Calories: 103 | Net Carbs: 22.1 g | Fat: 3.9 g |
Protein: 2.1 g

Ingredients:

- 1 C. raw, unsalted cashews soaked in water for 3 hours
- 1 T. pure vanilla extract
- 2 T. agave nectar
- 2 ½ C. water
- 1 C.:
  - Fresh strawberries – sliced
  - Fresh raspberries
  - Fresh blueberries

Technique:

1. Place soaked cashews in a high-power blender, along with ½ C. water, vanilla, and agave.
2. Blend on high for 2 minutes. Chill for at least 1 hour. This will also help stiffen the whipped cream.
3. Serve on top of fresh berries.

Vegan Dark Chocolate Mint Mousse

10 Min. to Get Ready | 4 Hr. Chill Time
Produces: 2 Servings
Nutritional Score: Calories: 662 | Net Carbs: 56.8 g | Fat: 58.9 g |
Protein: 17.1 g

Ingredients:

- 1½ C. coconut milk
- ¼ t. peppermint extract
- 6 T. unsweetened cacao powder
- 4 T. dark chocolate chips for garnish
- 1 T. maple syrup

Technique:

1. Whisk together all ingredients until little air bubbles start to appear.
2. Pour into 2 ramekins.
3. Place in fridge until set; allow up to 4 hours.
4. Top with dark chocolate chips before serving.

Raw Chocolate Brownies

20 Min. to Get Ready | 15 Min. Cook Time
Produces: 2 Servings
Nutritional Score: Calories: 175 | Net Carbs: 33.4 g | Fat: 5 g |
Protein: 2 g

Ingredients:

- ½ C. walnuts
- ½ C. almonds
- ¼ C. unsweetened cacao powder
- 1 C. dates
- 2 T. maple syrup

Technique:

1. Soak dates in water for about 10 minutes.
2. In a food processor, pulse nuts until a crumb-like consistency is attained.
3. Remove dates from water, drain, and wring out any excess water.
4. Add the dates, cacao powder, and maple syrup into the food processor. Blend until a smooth but thick consistency is reached.
5. On a piece of parchment paper, roll out brownie mixture into a rectangle, about 1 inch thick. Fold up in parchment paper and chill for 15 minutes.

Banana Almond Chia Pudding

10 Min. to Get Ready | 10 Min. to Cook
Produces: 3 Servings
Nutritional Score: Calories: 299 | Net Carbs: 21.6 g | Fat: 23.6 g |
Protein: 4.9 g

Ingredients:

- ¼ C. chia seeds
- 1 C. coconut milk
- 1 C. cashew milk
- 3 T. sliced almonds
- 3 bananas
- 1 t. ground cinnamon
- 2 T. maple syrup

Technique:

1. Whisk together cinnamon, maple syrup, and coconut milk until smooth. Add in chia seeds and let sit overnight.
2. Serve in cold dishes, each topped with one cut up banana and some sliced almonds.

Chocolate Chip Energy Bits

15 Min. to Get Ready | 4 Hr. Chill Time
Produces: 12 Bits
Nutritional Score: Calories: 100 | Net Carbs: 18.2 g | Fat: 2.2 g |
Protein: 2.7 g

Ingredients:

- ¼ C. maple syrup
- ¼ C. almond butter
- 1/3 C. mini dark chocolate chips
- 1 C. cooked quinoa
- 1 C. gluten-free oats
- ½ t. vanilla extract
- 1 t. cinnamon

Technique:

1. Knead all ingredients until a sticky dough forms and roll into small balls.
2. Place energy bits on a parchment-lined cookie sheet and refrigerate for 4 hours before serving.

Almond Butter Apple Slices

10 Min. to Get Ready | 5 Min. to Cook
Produces: 4 Servings
Nutritional Score: Calories: 114 | Net Carbs: 19.3 g | Fat: 4.7 g |
Protein: 1.7 g

Ingredients:

- 2 apples
- 2 T. dark chocolate chips
- ½ C. almond butter
- 2 T. slivered almonds
- 2 T. shredded coconut – unsweetened

Technique:

1. Remove the core of the apples and slice into rings.
2. Spread almond butter over one side and top with chocolate chips, slivered almonds, and coconut.

No-Bake Chocolate Cookie Dough Bars

15 Min. to Get Ready | 50 Min. Chill Time
Produces: 12 Servings
Nutritional Score: Calories: 341 | Net Carbs: 22 g | Fat: 27.1 g |
Protein: 6.1 g

Ingredients:

- ¾ C. dark chocolate chips
- 1 ½ C. almond flour
- 1 t. vanilla extract
- ½ C. maple syrup
- 5 T. nut butter of choice
- 2 ½ T. melted coconut oil

For the Chocolate Topping:

- ½ T. coconut oil
- 2 T. nut butter
- 1 C. dark chocolate chips

Technique:

1. Mix all listed bar ingredients.
2. In an 8-inch baking dish, firmly press dough evenly and place in the freezer for 30 minutes.
3. Melt all chocolate topping ingredients together, pour over the cookie dough bars, and place in the freezer for another 20 minutes.

Triple Berry Ice Cream

5 Min. to Get Ready | 3+ Hr. Chill Time
Produces: 6 Servings
Nutritional Score: Calories: 284 | Net Carbs: 25.2 g | Fat: 17.5 g |
Protein: 3 g

Ingredients:

- 1 C.:
  - Raspberries
  - Strawberries
  - Blueberries
- 3 ripe bananas
- 1 15-oz. can coconut milk

Technique:

1. Blend all ingredients.
2. Transfer to a freezer-safe container, cover, and freeze for 3
   hours.

Ginger Cookies with Cashew Vanilla Icing

15 Min. to Get Ready | 20 Min. to Cook
Produces: 16 cookies
Nutritional Score: Calories: 197 | Net Carbs: 17.9 g | Fat: 12.6 g |
Protein: 4.1 g

Ingredients:

- 1 ½ C. ground oats
- 3 mashed bananas
- ¼ t. sea salt
- 1 T. cinnamon
- 2 T. ground ginger

Cashew Vanilla Icing:

- 2 T. maple syrup
- 1 C. raw cashews – previously soaked for 3 hours
- 2 T. coconut oil
- 2 t. vanilla extract
- Water for blending

Technique:

1. Mix all dry ingredients together; add in the banana.
2. Spoon onto the cookie sheet and bake at 350°F for about 10-15 minutes. You will start to smell the banana when they are done.
3. Make the cashew vanilla icing by adding all ingredients to a blender. Place in the freezer to firm.
4. Let cookies cool completely before putting the icing.

Chapter 3: Smoothies

Blueberry Almond Smoothie

5 Min. to Get Ready | 5 Min. to Make
Produces: 2 Servings
Nutritional Score: Calories: 449 | Net Carbs: 38.7 g | Fat: 33 g |
Protein: 8.2 g

Ingredients:

- 1 ½ T. almond butter
- ¾ C. coconut milk
- ½ C. frozen blueberries
- 1 ½ ripe bananas
- 1 T. chia seed

Technique:

1. Using a high-speed blender, process all the listed ingredients until the consistency becomes smooth.
2. If the smoothie is too thick, add more milk until it thins out.

Green Mango Protein Smoothie

5 Min. to Get Ready | 5 Min. to Make
Produces: 2 Servings
Nutritional Score: Calories: 634 | Net Carbs: 56 g | Fat: 47.2 g |
Protein: 8.6 g

Ingredients:

- 1 C. spinach
- 2 apples
- 2 C. chopped mango
- ½-inch peeled fresh ginger
- 1 ½ C. almond milk
- 1 T. hemp seed

Technique:

1. Blend all the listed ingredients. Add some ice if you would like to make it colder.
2. If the smoothie is too thick, add more almond milk.

Strawberry Banana Smoothie

5 Min. to Get Ready | 5 Min. to Make
Produces: 2 Servings
Nutritional Score: Calories: 114 | Net Carbs: 26.6 g | Fat: 1.2 g |
Protein: 2 g

Ingredients:

- 1 ripe banana
- 2 C. fresh strawberries
- ½ C. dairy-free milk of choice
- Ice – if desired

Technique:

1. Blend all the ingredients together.

Hemp Oatmeal Chocolate Smoothie

5 Min. to Get Ready | 5 Min. to Make
Produces: 2 Servings
Nutritional Score: Calories: 415 | Net Carbs: 56 g | Fat: 23 g |
Protein: 20.2 g

Ingredients:

- 1 ripe banana
- 4 T. cacao powder – unsweetened
- 2 T. maple syrup
- 1 C. coconut milk
- ½ C. water
- 4 T. hemp seeds – shelled
- 1 T. oats

Technique:

1. Blend all ingredients on high setting until a smooth consistency is reached.
2. Add more milk if the smoothie is too thick.
3. Add ice if you would like to make it colder.

Vanilla Cashew Smoothie

5 Min. to Get Ready | 5 Min. to Make
Produces: 1 Serving
Nutritional Score: Calories: 569 | Net Carbs: 68 g | Fat: 30.3 g |
Protein: 13 g

Ingredients:

- 1/3 C. raw cashews
- 1 banana
- 1 T. chia seeds
- 1 T. maple syrup
- 1 t. vanilla extract OR 1 vanilla bean
- 1/3 C. water
- 1 C. ice

Technique:

1. Blend all ingredients until smooth.
2. Add more water if needed.

Lavender Blueberry Smoothie

5 Min. to Get Ready | 5 Min. to Make
Produces: 2 Servings
Nutritional Score: Calories: 479 | Net Carbs: 34.4 g | Fat: 39 g |
Protein: 5.2 g

Ingredients:

- ½ C. ice
- ½ C. chard
- 1 C. fresh blueberries
- 1 C. unsweetened coconut milk
- ½ avocado
- ½ banana
- 1 T. culinary lavender
- 1 t. pure vanilla extract

Technique:

1. Blend everything until smooth and creamy.

Avocado Kale & Raspberry Smoothie

5 Min. to Get Ready | 5 Min. to Make
Produces: 2 Servings
Nutritional Score: Calories: 627 | Net Carbs: 47 g | Fat: 49 g |
Protein: 10.4 g

Ingredients:

- 1 handful of kale
- ½ avocado
- 1 C. almond milk
- 1 C. raspberries
- 1 banana
- 1 T. maple syrup
- 2 T. nut butter
- 1 T. flax seed

Technique:

1. Run all ingredients on the blender's high setting until the consistency is smooth.
2. Add ice if you would like to make the smoothie colder.

Tropical Acai Smoothie

5 Min. to Get Ready | 5 Min. to Make
Produces: 1 Serving
Nutritional Score: Calories: 584 | Net Carbs: 77.4 g | Fat: 33 g | Protein: 6.2 g

Ingredients:

- 1 packet acai puree
- 1 banana
- ¾ C. blueberries
- ½ mango
- ½ C. coconut milk
- ½ C. water

Technique:

1. Blend everything together and enjoy!

Green Avocado Smoothie

5 Min. to Get Ready | 5 Min. to Make
Produces: 2 Servings
Nutritional Score: Calories: 369 | Net Carbs: 18.7 g | Fat: 33.9 g | Protein: 3.3 g

Ingredients:

- 1 avocado
- 1 tbsp. maple syrup
- ½ C. almond milk

Technique:

1. Blend all ingredients together.
2. Add more milk if the smoothie is too thick.

Superfood Smoothie

5 Min. to Get Ready | 5 Min. to Make
Produces: 2 Servings
Nutritional Score: Calories: 333 | Net Carbs: 30.8 g | Fat: 24.7 g |
Protein: 4 g

Ingredients:

- ¼ C. cucumber
- ½ avocado
- 1 C. spinach
- 1 kiwi
- 1 green apple
- 1 celery stalk
- 2 sprigs mint
- ½ C. coconut milk
- ½ C. water
- Handful of ice

Technique:

1. Blend everything on high; add more water if necessary.

Energizing Kale Smoothie

5 Min. to Get Ready | 5 Min. to Make
Produces: 2 Servings
Nutritional Score: Calories: 190 | Net Carbs: 34.7 g | Fat: 5 g |
Protein: 4.5 g

Ingredients:

- 1 ¼ C. fresh kale
- 1 peeled carrot
- 1 banana
- ½ green apple
- 1 T. chia seeds
- ½ C. cashew milk
- ½ C. water

Technique:

1. Blend everything; add more ice if necessary.

Refreshing Pineapple Protein Smoothie

5 Min. to Get Ready | 5 Min. to Make
Produces: 2 Servings
Nutritional Score: Calories: 550 | Net Carbs: 56 g | Fat: 34.2 g |
Protein: 14 g

Ingredients:

- 1 C. spinach
- 1 C. fresh pineapple
- 1 kiwi
- 1 C. fresh mango
- 1 orange
- 1/4 C. raw cashews
- 2 T. hemp seed
- 1 T. chia seed
- ½ C. coconut milk

Technique:

1. Blend everything; add water if the smoothie is too thick.
2. Add ice if you would like to make it colder.

Purple Antioxidant Smoothie

5 Min. to Get Ready | 5 Min. to Make
Produces: 2 Servings
Nutritional Score: Calories: 372 | Net Carbs: 46.1 g | Fat: 20.6 g |
Protein: 5.7 g

Ingredients:

- 1 C. mixed berries
- 1 packet acai puree
- 1 banana
- 1 beet
- 3 seeded dates
- ½ C. almond milk
- 1 T. chia seeds
- ½ C. water

Technique:

1. Blend all ingredients on high until smooth.
2. Add more water to thin out the smoothie if needed.
3. Add ice if needed.

Chapter 4: Salads

Berry Quinoa Salad

15 Min. to Get Ready | 25 Min. to Make
Produces: 6 Servings
Nutritional Score: Calories: 446 | Net Carbs: 38.9 g | Fat: 28.5 g |
Protein: 14.7 g

Ingredients:

- 1 C. cooked quinoa
- 2 C. blueberries
- 2 C. strawberries
- 6 C. spinach
- 2 cubed avocados
- 1 T. hemp seed – per bowl
- ½ C. walnuts
- 2 T. Dijon mustard
- 1 lemon

Technique:

1. In each bowl, start with a bed of spinach; add on a scoop of quinoa, berries, avocado, a sprinkle of hemp seeds, and toss on a few walnuts.
2. Combine Dijon mustard and lemon juice to make the dressing.
3. Drizzle the dressing on top of each salad.

Mandarin Kale Salad with Sweet Tahini Dressing

10 Min. to Get Ready | 15 Min. to Make
Produces: 3 Servings
Nutritional Score: Calories: 550 | Net Carbs: 38 g | Fat: 43.6 g | Protein: 11 g

Ingredients:

- 3 mandarin oranges
- 1 bunch roughly chopped kale
- ½ C. dried cranberries
- ½ C. pecans

Dressing:

- Juice from 1 large orange
- 2 T. tahini
- 1 T. sesame oil
- ½ T. apple cider vinegar

Technique:

1. Combine all ingredients for the dressing and set aside.
2. Prepare each salad by starting with a bed of kale.
3. Each salad will get 1 mandarin.
4. Sprinkle the salads with dried cranberries and pecans.
5. Drizzle with dressing.

Thai Zucchini Noodle Salad

15 Min. to Get Ready | 15 Min. to Make
Produces: 2 Servings
Nutritional Score: Calories: 355 | Net Carbs: 43 g | Fat: 17 g |
Protein: 20 g

Ingredients:

- 3 shredded carrots
- 2 spiralized zucchinis – drained of water
- 2 thinly sliced bell peppers
- 10 oz. sliced mushrooms
- 2 t. minced garlic
- ¼ C. peanut butter
- 2 t. freshly grated ginger
- 3 T. liquid aminos
- 1 t. sriracha
- 1 t. maple syrup

Technique:

1. Combine zucchini and carrots; set aside.
2. Make Thai dressing by combining peanut butter, liquid aminos, sriracha, maple syrup, ginger, and garlic together. Whisk well to combine. Add a little hot water to smooth out the dressing.
3. Sauté peppers and mushrooms for about 5 minutes and set aside.
4. Toss all ingredients together; top with dressing.

Tomato Avocado Onion Salad

10 Min. to Get Ready | 10 Min. to Make
Produces: 2 Servings
Nutritional Score: Calories: 613 | Net Carbs: 37 g | Fat: 54 g |
Protein: 8 g

Ingredients:

- 2 diced avocados
- ½ sliced red onion
- 1 lb. cherry tomatoes
- 1 cucumber
- ¼ C. chopped fresh cilantro
- Juice from 1 lemon
- 2 T. cold-pressed olive oil
- Salt and pepper

Technique:

1. In a prepared bowl, throw together all the ingredients and
   drizzle with lemon juice and oil.

Watermelon & Jasmine Rice Salad

15 Min. to Get Ready | 25 Min. to Make
Produces: 2 Servings
Nutritional Score: Calories: 555 | Net Carbs: 99.9 g | Fat: 14.6 g |
Protein: 8.3 g

Ingredients:

- ½ C. coconut milk
- 1 C. cut up watermelon
- ½ C. fresh blueberries
- ½ C. chopped fresh basil
- 1 C. cooked jasmine rice
- 2 T. maple syrup
- 1 C. spinach

Technique:

1. Cook jasmine rice according to package directions. Once the rice has cooled, stir in coconut milk and maple syrup.
2. Chop watermelon and basil. Set aside.
3. Lay down a bed of spinach and spoon rice into bowls; add in watermelon, basil, and blueberries.

Mango Black Bean Salad

10 Min. to Get Ready | 10 Min. to Make
Produces: 3 Servings
Nutritional Score: Calories: 669 | Net Carbs: 136.9 g | Fat: 2.8 g |
Protein: 33.4 g

Ingredients:

- 2 peeled and diced mangoes
- 3 peeled mandarins
- 1 diced bell pepper
- 1 bunch thinly sliced green onions
- 1 seeded and finely diced jalapeno
- ½ C. chopped fresh cilantro
- 1 C. cleaned black beans
- 1 C. cleaned white beans
- 2 C. arugula
- Juice from 1 lemon
- Juice from 1 orange

Technique:

1. Combine all ingredients together. Each bowl will get 1 tangerine.
2. Squeeze juice from the lemon and orange over the salad.

Red Apple & Kale Salad

10 Min. to Get Ready | 10 Min. to Make
Produces: 5 Servings
Nutritional Score: Calories: 261 | Net Carbs: 26.6 g | Fat: 17.8 g |
Protein: 4 g

Ingredients:

- 3 thinly sliced apples
- 2 chopped bunches kale
- ½ C. slivered almonds
- ½ C. coconut flakes

Lemon Dressing:

- Juice from 1 lemon
- 1 minced garlic clove
- 1 t. Dijon mustard
- ¼ C. cold-pressed oil of choice
- Salt and pepper

Technique:

1. Make the lemon dressing by combining all ingredients and whisking until smooth. Set aside.
2. Prepare all salad ingredients; top with dressing and toss to combine.

Cauliflower & Chickpea Salad

15 Min. to Get Ready | 10 Min. to Make
Produces: 4 Servings
Nutritional Score: Calories: 704 | Net Carbs: 89.5 g | Fat: 32.6 g |
Protein: 23.4 g

Ingredients:

- 1 head cauliflower – cut into florets
- 1 thinly sliced apple
- 2 cut and cubed avocados
- 1 t. chili powder
- 1 thinly sliced shallot
- 1 handful chopped cilantro
- 1 handful chopped mint
- 1 14-oz. can clean chickpeas
- Salt and pepper

Technique:

1. In your food processor, pulse the cauliflower until its consistency has become rice-like.
2. Toss all ingredients together with a little olive oil and fresh lime juice.

Strawberry Mango and Pineapple Tacos

15 Min. to Get Ready | 5 Min. to Make
Produces: 2 Servings
Nutritional Score: Calories: 452 | Net Carbs: 68.6 g | Fat: 21.6 g |
Protein: 8 g

Ingredients:

- 1 C. sliced strawberries
- 1 C. freshly cut up pineapple
- 1 cubed mango
- 1 C. cherry tomatoes
- 1 avocado
- Romaine lettuce leaves
- ¼ C. chopped and soaked red onion
- 1 handful chopped cilantro
- 1 small handful chopped basil
- Juice from 1 lime
- Salt and pepper

Technique:

1. Place romaine leaves on a serving platter.
2. In a small bowl, combine strawberries, pineapple, mango, tomatoes, and herbs. Set aside.
3. In another bowl, mash avocado with onion, lime juice, salt, and pepper. Keep the avocado chunky.
4. Spread a spoonful of the avocado mix on each romaine leaf.
5. Top with fruit mix.

Rainbow Beet Salad

10 Min. to Get Ready | 15 Min. to Make
Produces: 3 Servings
Nutritional Score: Calories: 615 | Net Carbs: 46.8 g | Fat: 44.5 g |
Protein: 18.3 g

Ingredients:

- 1 C. spinach
- 1 C. cooked edamame
- 1 cubed avocado
- 1 sliced beet
- 1 sliced bell pepper
- 1 peeled and grated carrot
- 1 C. arugula
- 1 C. fresh blueberries
- ½ C. slivered almonds

Technique:

1. To make the dressing, combine all ingredients and place in the fridge to keep cool.
2. Toast almonds on the stove top until browned.
3. Combine all salad ingredients and top with freshly squeezed lemon juice.

Walnut & Pear Salad with Lemon Poppy Seed Dressing

15 Min. to Get Ready | 10 Min. to Make
Produces: 4 Servings
Nutritional Score: Calories: 408 | Net Carbs: 32.6 g | Fat: 30 g |
Protein: 10.1 g

Ingredients:

- 2 sliced pears
- 4 C. spinach
- 1 cubed avocado
- ½ C. dried cranberries
- 1 C. walnuts

Lemon Poppy Seed Dressing:

- 3 T. avocado oil
- 3 T. cold water
- 1 t. Dijon mustard
- ½ t. onion powder
- ¼ t. lemon zest
- Juice from 2 lemons
- 1 T. poppy seeds
- 1 T. maple syrup
- ¼ t. sea salt

Technique:

1. Whisk together all the dressing ingredients and chill until salad is ready.
2. Toss all the salad ingredients together and top with dressing.

White Bean & Asparagus Salad

10 Min. to Get Ready | 15 Min. to Make
Produces: 2 Servings
Nutritional Score: Calories: 600 | Net Carbs: 50.2 g | Fat: 39.6 g |
Protein: 18 g

Ingredients:

- ½ C. cleaned white beans
- ½ pound cut and blanched asparagus
- 1 cubed avocado
- 1 chopped bell pepper
- ¼ C. chopped parsley
- 1 t. dried oregano
- 2 C. arugula

Dressing:

- ½ T. cold-pressed olive oil
- 1 T. fresh lemon juice
- 1 T. Dijon mustard
- Salt and pepper

Technique:

1. Combine all ingredients for the dressing and store in the fridge until ready to use.
2. Blanch the asparagus by boiling for 3-5 minutes until tender. Run under cold water once done.
3. Toss all the salad ingredients together and serve on top of the arugula.
4. Drizzle with dressing.

3 Bean Salad with Roasted Sweet Potatoes

20 Min. to Get Ready | 30 Min. to Make
Produces: 2 Servings
Nutritional Score: Calories: 906 | Net Carbs: 135 g | Fat: 30.8 g |
Protein: 30.4 g

Ingredients:

- 1/3 C.:
  o White beans
  o Pinto beans
  o Black beans
- 1-pound peeled and diced sweet potatoes
- 1 diced red onion
- ½ C. cilantro
- 1 minced garlic clove
- ¼ C. pumpkin seeds
- Juice from 1 lime
- 1 t. chili powder
- ¼ t. sea salt
- Cold-pressed oil

Technique:

1. Preheat your oven to 400°F.
2. Toss sweet potatoes and onions with 1 T. of oil. Bake until sweet potatoes are at the desired tenderness. This will take about 35 minutes.
3. Mix together lime juice, garlic clove, chili powder, sea salt, and 1 T. of oil to make the dressing.
4. Rinse and drain the beans.
5. Once the sweet potatoes and onions are done, transfer to a large bowl. Combine with beans, cilantro, and pumpkin seeds.
6. Drizzle with dressing.

Conclusion

I hope you enjoyed your copy of *The Complete Plant-Based Cookbook*. Let's hope it was informative and that it provided you with a good foundation of recipes that will allow you to easily live the plant-based diet lifestyle.

** Remember to use your link to claim your 3 FREE Cookbooks on Health, Fitness & Dieting Instantly

https://bit.ly/2MkqTit

Made in the USA
Columbia, SC
13 February 2019